W9-AOR-893

—

THE 1964
FREEDOM
SUMMER

THE 1964
FREEDOM
SUMMER

BY REBECCA FELIX

CONTENT CONSULTANT
ROBERT W. WIDELL JR., PHD
ASSISTANT PROFESSOR OF AFRICAN-AMERICAN,
CIVIL RIGHTS, & RECENT AMERICAN HISTORY
UNIVERSITY OF RHODE ISLAND

ABDO
Publishing Company

CREDITS

Published by ABDO Publishing Company, PO Box 398166, Minneapolis, MN 55439. Copyright © 2014 by Abdo Consulting Group, Inc. International copyrights reserved in all countries. No part of this book may be reproduced in any form without written permission from the publisher. The Essential Library™ is a trademark and logo of ABDO Publishing Company.

Printed in the United States of America,
North Mankato, Minnesota
102013
012014

Editor: Susan E. Hamen
Series Designer: Becky Daum

Photo credits: Bettmann/Corbis/AP Images, cover, 2; Bettmann/Corbis, 6, 13, 14, 22, 25, 53, 84; FBI/AP Images, 8; Bill Hudson/AP Images, 26; Jack Moebes/Corbis, 30; Steve Schapiro/Corbis, 37, 38, 46, 48, 61, 68; Bob Adelman/Corbis, 43; Ted Polumbaum/PR Newswire/AP Images, 50; Jack Thornell/AP Images, 57, 73; AP Images, 58, 78, 80; BH/AP Images, 67; Rogelio Solis/AP Images, 95

Library of Congress Control Number: 2013946959

Cataloging-in-Publication Data

Felix, Rebecca, 1984-
The 1964 Freedom Summer / Rebecca Felix.
   p. cm. -- (Essential events)
Includes bibliographical references and index.
ISBN 978-1-62403-256-1
1. Mississippi Freedom Project--Juvenile literature. 2. Civil rights movements--Mississippi--History--20th century--Juvenile literature. 3. Civil rights workers--Mississippi--History--20th century--Juvenile literature. 4. African Americans--Civil rights--Mississippi--History--20th century--Juvenile literature. 5. African Americans--Suffrage--Mississippi--History--20th century--Juvenile literature. I. Title.
323--dc23

2013946959

CONTENTS

DEC 1 3 2014

MISSING

THE FBI IS SEEKING INFORMATION CONCERNING THE DISAPPEARANCE
PHILADELPHIA, MISSISSIPPI, OF THESE THREE INDIVIDUALS ON JUNE 21, 1964. EXTEN
INVESTIGATION IS BEING CONDUCTED TO LOCATE GOODMAN, CHANEY, AND SCHWER
WHO ARE DESCRIBED AS FOLLOWS:

ANDREW GOODMAN	JAMES EARL CHANEY	MICHAEL HENRY SCHWE

RACE:	White	Negro	White
SEX:	Male	Male	Male
DOB:	November 23, 1943	May 30, 1943	November 6, 1939
POB:	New York City	Meridian, Mississippi	New York City
AGE:	20 years	21 years	24 years
HEIGHT:	5'10"	5'7"	5'9" to 5'10"
WEIGHT:	150 pounds	135 to 140 pounds	170 to 180 pounds
HAIR:	Dark brown; wavy	Black	Brown
EYES:	Brown	Brown	Light blue
TEETH:		Good: none missing	
SCAR	RKS	ar 2 inches above left ear.	Pock mark center of forehead, slight s on bridge of nose, appendectomy sc broken leg scar.

SHOULD YOU HAVE OR IN THE FUTURE RECEIVE ANY INFORMATIO
CO THE EABO S HESE INDIVIDUALS, YOU A
RE STED O E O HE AREST OFFICE OF THE FBI.
T HONE N B S EL

CHAPTER ONE

DIRECTOR
FEDERAL BUREAU OF INVESTIGATION
UNITED STATES DEPARTMENT OF

SUMMER VICTIMS

The summer sun blazed overhead. The air was thick and stagnant, dripping with humidity. By afternoon, a reeking smell wafted from a trench dug by Federal Bureau of Investigation (FBI) agents. That morning, August 4, 1964, agents first used a steam shovel and bulldozer to plow the earth at the dam in Neshoba County, Mississippi. As the initial pit was dug, the smell was unleashed. It was a sure sign something—or someone—was decaying below the dirt.

The agents switched to handheld shovels and carefully hacked away the earth. Suddenly, a boot emerged. An agent crawled from the deep pit and vomited. More body parts of three young men were uncovered: legs, hands, and torsos. The men's bodies, two white and one black, were buried haphazardly on top of and next to one another. They had been decomposing for more than six weeks—since the first night of Freedom Summer, a campaign launched to seek equality for black Mississippians. The men had been

Freedom Summer volunteers Andrew Goodman, James Chaney, and Michael Schwerner were missing for 44 days. The FBI met resistance in Mississippi during their search.

More than six weeks after the men went missing, the bodies of
Chaney, Goodman, and Schwerner were finally unearthed.

workers on the campaign—and they had become its
first victims.

The murdered young men, Michael "Mickey"
Schwerner, Andrew Goodman, and James "JE"
Chaney, had become targets for white segregationists
in Mississippi who despised Freedom Summer and
its volunteers. Through the campaign, college youth
from across the nation flooded the state to work
alongside black Mississippians engaged in efforts to
seize the basic rights they deserved as citizens but had
long been denied, such as the rights to vote and earn a
proper education.

The nation grieved and was outraged over the gruesome murders of the three volunteers. But in Mississippi, racial hate crimes were nothing new. And even murder often was not enough to send those guilty to jail—at least not if they were white.

Mayhem in Mississippi

In the 1960s, it had been approximately 100 years since slavery was abolished in the United States. But racial

SCHWERNER, GOODMAN, AND CHANEY

Kind and easygoing, 24-year-old Michael "Mickey" Schwerner moved to Mississippi from New York City with his new wife, Rita, in the spring of 1964. Schwerner was a college graduate with a degree in social work and was dedicated to civil rights for black Americans. He and Rita would often attend demonstrations, where the couple sometimes got arrested for protesting segregation.

Andrew Goodman was also from New York City. His family had instilled in him social values of equality and a will to fight injustice. Twenty-year-old Goodman was passionately interested in the plights of the underprivileged and abused.

When he heard of a new venture that aimed to give aid to black Mississippians plagued with racial discrimination and violence, Goodman eagerly signed up. The Schwerners did as well.

Deep in the heart of Mississippi, in the small town of Meridian, lived James "JE" Chaney. Born and raised in the South, Chaney, who was black, had been surrounded by the bitter hatred and tension between Mississippi's black and white communities his entire life. In 1963, Chaney became involved with the Congress of Racial Equality (CORE). He was a volunteer in the 1964 summer civil rights campaign in Mississippi, where he met white workers Schwerner and Goodman.

discrimination, oppression, and violence persisted to varying degrees. Treatment of black citizens remained unequal. In addition, black citizens across the South had long been disenfranchised, their right to vote systematically stripped away. While legally allowed to vote under US law, black citizens in the South were met with extreme opposition when they tried to do so.

Blacks were treated as second-class citizens in virtually all aspects of life in Southern states. Jim Crow was a system of white supremacy that gave whites economic, political, and social power through use of harassment, intimidation, and violence.

Segregation was another way whites maintained power through Jim Crow laws. Blacks and whites went to different schools and churches and lived in isolated neighborhoods. They dined, shopped for groceries, and even sat on buses separately.

UNWELCOME IN MISSISSIPPI

Many—including local law enforcement officials—expressed their contempt for the campaign, the missing men, and the FBI for being involved. It was expressed to FBI agents the white community believed the trio of missing men had taken off on their own in some sort of publicity stunt, and that the FBI should follow suit and disappear. Others assumed from the beginning the three men were murdered by local whites, and warned that it was likely not going to be the only case of murder Freedom Summer would cause.

In general, the separate facilities and institutions for blacks were second-rate.

Whites used brutal violence to enforce their supremacy. Blacks who opposed discrimination and segregation, or those who tried to exercise their rights as citizens by voting or registering to vote, were harassed, beaten, or murdered. Blacks who sought equality were also punished economically. Some blacks lost their homes or businesses, were denied loans, or had buyers refuse to buy their wares or crops. Mississippi was home to some of the worst cases of injustice, becoming what one historian described as a "symbol of racial terror."[1]

Freedom Summer

Since 1960, the Student Nonviolent Coordinating Committee (SNCC), a civil rights organization, was interested in developing voter rights projects in Mississippi. That year, less than 2 percent of black Mississippian adults were registered to vote.[2] In the years following, SNCC enacted small voter registration projects in Mississippi. In certain counties there, although blacks made up more than half the population, not one was allowed to vote.

With previous efforts largely unsuccessful, a bigger, longer campaign was formed. SNCC called to action hundreds of youth from across the nation to storm the state the following summer for the Mississippi Freedom Project, or Freedom Summer. The main goal of Freedom Summer was to force the nation to pay attention to what was happening in Mississippi, namely the lack of response to murders of and brutality against blacks. The nation largely ignored the plight of black Mississippians. But Freedom Summer organizers knew white students willing to risk their safety to get involved would draw the media's attention.

Freedom Summer supporters protested the violence against volunteers through picketing and sit-ins. At times, they were joined by passersby.

The long-term goals of the project were to aid black Mississippians in bettering their circumstances and overcoming white intimidation and discrimination. Working to aid blacks in successfully registering to vote and cast ballots was a major tool in working toward these goals. Improving the lacking education Mississippi provided its black youth was another major goal. Volunteers and organizers prepared for the peaceful assault for approximately six months. Anticipation of their arrival increased racial tensions in Mississippi. White residents prepared for what they felt was an invasion. The project would challenge ideologies that had been in place for more than a century.

CHAPTER
TWO

FROM SLAVERY TO CIVIL RIGHTS

F rom the 1400s through the 1700s, countless Africans were captured as slaves and transported to European countries and colonies. Slaves were sold for profit and treated as property. The practice of slavery was established throughout the future United States. Although some people began to morally oppose slavery in the late 1700s, slavery wouldn't be abolished until following the Civil War (1861–1865). However, even with this new freedom from slavery, black Americans, particularly in the South, would endure an oppressive system of social, economic, and political discrimination that would limit their freedoms and rights for another century.

Segregation

During the late 1800s, white supremacists in the South enacted Jim Crow laws. These encompassed a complex

Before slavery was abolished in 1865, many blacks spent their entire lives enslaved and forced to do hard labor.

system of political, social, and economic laws and conduct to keep white and black people separate. Blacks were kept in a position of lesser power in every aspect of life. The Jim Crow laws were enforced through brutal violence, or the threat of it. Black people were not allowed to use the same public facilities, live in the same neighborhoods, or attend the same schools as whites. Facilities designated for blacks were almost always lacking or completely inadequate. Many blacks immediately opposed Jim Crow laws and reacted with resistance.

Segregation gained federal backing in 1896, in the Supreme Court case *Plessy v. Ferguson*. Four years earlier, in 1892, Louisianan Homer Plessy boarded a train in New Orleans and sat in the whites-only section. Plessy had light skin and resembled a white person, but he was one-eighth black and announced himself as such. The conductor demanded Plessy move. When he refused, Plessy was arrested and charged with disobeying the state's Separate Car Act. The case was examined by the US Supreme Court, which ruled on May 18, 1896, that "separate but equal" segregation of blacks and whites was constitutional. Black resistance to Jim Crow segregation and discrimination continued through boycotts and demonstrations into the early 1900s.

Southern communities remained separated, but blacks were still not provided with equal facilities or opportunities. Several states also enacted laws and rewrote state constitutions that effectively kept black citizens from voting, although it was their federal right to do so. On November 1, 1890, the new Mississippi Constitution declared citizens would be required to pass literacy and "understanding" tests to be eligible to vote. These tests were considered purposefully difficult or impossible to pass, and they kept the majority of Southern blacks from voting for decades.

Jim Crow Violence

Violence was another component of racial injustice. Blacks were victims of constant harassment and attack. Some were killed in gruesome ways, often for trivial reasons, or no reason at all, other than for whites to retain supremacy and power.

This violence was especially inflicted on blacks who fought against injustice and tried to advance themselves. White segregationists formed organized groups throughout the South. The most violent and well-known of these groups was the Ku Klux Klan (KKK), founded in 1865. KKK membership grew to an all-time high in the 1920s, when the organization's worst reign of terror occurred.

White society was also responsible for entrenching Jim Crow. White businessmen and landowners, law enforcement, and citizens used violence and harassment to keep blacks in a lower status.

Several groups opposing segregation and discrimination also formed in the early to mid-1900s. In 1909, the National Association for the Advancement of Colored People (NAACP), an organization working to provide equality for black Americans in areas such as voting, housing, and employment, was established. The Congress of Racial Equality (CORE), an organization aimed at ending racial discrimination through demonstrations and projects, was founded in 1942. During and after World War II (1939–1945), there was an uprising of black resistance across the nation. NAACP branches grew, and thousands of blacks registered to vote. But segregation and discrimination stubbornly plagued much of the country.

KU KLUX KLAN

The Ku Klux Klan (KKK) formed in 1865 in Tennessee. The KKK is a white supremacist organization, meaning it believes white people are superior to other races. Membership was traditionally kept secret. Members wore white, hooded sheets to keep their identities hidden. But many KKK members in the 1960s were proud to belong and made their involvement well-known. The organization waged violent war through beatings, bombings, and scare tactics, such as placing massive burning crosses on the lawns of black homes.

Civil Rights Movement

In the mid-1950s, another uprising began. Black Americans had established a platform of people and organizations supporting activism in prior decades. Additionally, their involvement in World War II made the US government slightly more receptive to their efforts for equality, which made the timing right for a push to action.

Historians debate which events marked the beginning of the modern civil rights movement. Some look to May 17, 1954, when the US Supreme Court overturned its ruling of "separate but equal" in schools. Many were outraged by the decision, especially white Southerners.

Others pinpoint 1955 as the official start of the civil rights movement. On May 31, the Supreme Court determined in the *Brown II* decision that schools were to be desegregated with "all deliberate speed."[2] On November 7, the US Supreme Court declared segregation in public recreational facilities unconstitutional.

Several black activists worked to bring segregation to the national spotlight leading up to and after these decisions. Charles Hamilton Houston, who became the first special counsel of the National Association for the Advancement of Colored People (NAACP) in the 1930s, and his protégé, Thurgood Marshall, played a role in getting the Supreme Court to acknowledge and deal with segregation using the US court system. Marshall succeeded Houston as the NAACP special counsel in the 1940s. He continued challenging black inequality, which led to the Supreme Court declaring public segregation unconstitutional.

Outraged by the Supreme Court's decision to desegregate public facilities, branches of White Citizens Councils formed. Members opposed integration, and some attacked blacks involved in campaigning for voting rights. Blacks who even attempted to register or resisted discrimination by joining a black rights organization were threatened or violently punished.

In December 1955, a major boycott of the Montgomery, Alabama, bus system began when black passenger Rosa Parks was arrested for refusing to give up her seat for white passengers. The boycott lasted

Rosa Parks made history in 1956 when she refused to give up her seat at the front of a bus in Montgomery, Alabama.

more than one year and led to the successful integration of Montgomery buses.

The Movement Reaches Mississippi

Mississippi was a leader in resistance to desegregation. However, a tragedy occurred within the state in 1955 that was horrific enough to strengthen the resolve of outside activists to insist on action in Mississippi. On August 24, black 14-year-old Emmett Till was gruesomely murdered in Money, Mississippi, for flirtatiously saying hello to a white woman. Till's mother requested that her son's casket be open during his funeral. Photos were published of Till's corpse to show the extent of his injuries. When Till's white murderers were acquitted, outrage erupted in black communities. Both blacks and whites were moved to join the fight for black civil rights, even in Mississippi, which had until then remained virtually unchanged by

THE CIVIL RIGHTS MOVEMENT BEGINS WITH NONVIOLENT PROTEST

Between its start in the mid-1950s and its end in the 1960s, several events were significant in shaping the civil rights movement. In December 1955, Rosa Parks was arrested in Montgomery, Alabama, for refusing to give up her seat on a bus to white passengers. Days later, the black citizens of Montgomery, who made up a large portion of the city's passengers, staged a boycott of the city buses that lasted more than one year. In 1957, nine black students, known as the Little Rock Nine, enrolled in and entered a Little Rock, Arkansas, high school despite angry white mobs that gathered outside. On February 1, 1960, four black students sat at a lunch counter that was for whites only at Woolworth's store and restaurant in Greensboro, North Carolina. Workers refused to serve the students. The students refused to move. The students returned day after day to demonstrate with nonviolent sit-ins. Blacks would sit stoically in the face of violent reactions to their sit-ins. Some did not move when angry segregationists burned them with lit cigarettes or doused them with ketchup at lunch counters. Although not new, the sit-in tactic became a powerful tool of protest in the movement thereafter. Soon, nonviolent protest by sit-in was common across the country.

the blossoming movement. As NAACP leader Amzie Moore recalled of the Till murder and trial, "From that point on, Mississippi began to move."[3] Till's death emphasized to black Mississippians, as one historian put it, that "little had changed in Mississippi, and that everything had to."[4]

As the civil rights movement gained steam, countless protests, marches, sit-ins, and meetings took place. The movement was largely focused on tactics or strategies of nonviolent resistance, but these demonstrations were often met with violence from segregationists. While there were a handful of passionate, charismatic civil rights leaders during the movement, the everyday work of masses of citizens played a key role in the movement's success. Author Charles Payne wrote of SNCC leader Robert "Bob" Moses's idea that the civil rights movement successfully employed two traditions. The first tradition was mobilizing the community, which was used for short-terms goals or events, such as large public demonstrations. The second tradition, which revolved around organization, was especially influential to Freedom Summer. As Payne explained Moses's thoughts,

> The Mississippi movement reflects another tradition of Black activism, one of community organizing, a

Segregation in schools was declared unconstitutional in 1954. Schools across the nation began integrating black and white students, but a decade later, Mississippi had not yet desegregated its schools.

tradition with a different sense of what freedom means and therefore a greater emphasis on the long-term development of leadership in ordinary men and women.[5]

Civil rights activists won small victories and inched toward progress in the 1950s, but the battle was far from over. As the 1960s dawned, the South remained embroiled in conflict, with some states, such as Mississippi, faring worse than others.

CHAPTER
THREE

TARGETING MISSISSIPPI

B y the early 1960s, the civil rights movement had not had much impact on conditions for black Mississippians. The state had the highest rates of poverty and illiteracy in the nation. These conditions were worse in black communities. In 1960, 86 percent of nonwhite Mississippi families lived below national poverty levels.[1] Black Mississippians completed just five years of school on average. Lack of decent education and educational funding created an economic cycle blacks could not escape. Even if blacks overcame poor educational opportunities and developed the skills to gain better jobs, whites often refused to hire them.

Racial violence permeated Mississippi culture. As author Bruce Watson summarized, in the early 1960s, black corpses floating in Mississippi rivers were "as common as a snake."[2] Chaos erupted at the slightest everyday infractions. Integrating white facilities incited

Picketers showed support for black voter registration in Greenwood, Mississippi, in March 1964.

27

BLACK POVERTY AND EDUCATION IN MISSISSIPPI

The median income of a nonwhite family in Mississippi in 1960 was just $1,444—lower than anywhere else in the country.[3] That same year, two-thirds of black Mississippi homes were without toilets and deemed to be "deteriorating."[4] Black schools and black students received far less funding than white students. In 1964, the state spent more than $80 on each white student and a little over $20 on each black student.[5] Rural areas fared even worse: in Holly Bluff, Mississippi, the state spent an average of $191.70 on each white student but only $1.26 on each black student.[6]

white aggression and violence. A riot in Biloxi, Mississippi, on April 24, 1960, for example, began when black citizens attempted to attend a beach reserved for whites, and it ended in the shooting of two whites and eight blacks.

Registering to vote, or even showing interest in doing so, was also an invitation for attack. If blacks made it inside courthouses to register, discriminatory roadblocks awaited them. Blacks had to pay poll taxes or take unfair literacy tests to register. When blacks did manage to register, they often became the victims of social, economic, or physical attack, and even murder, for doing so.

SNCC Voter Registration Drives

Black rights organizations, including SNCC, were frustrated that violence and discrimination had not waned in Mississippi through civil rights movement efforts. In 1960, Moses traveled to Mississippi as an SNCC representative and spoke with NAACP leader Moore about the intense ongoing oppression and discrimination in Mississippi.

During their visit, Moore told Moses he believed securing voting rights would be the biggest influence in ending discrimination in Mississippi. This conversation planted the first seeds of a campaign that would change Mississippi—and the nation—in coming years.

Beginning in 1961, SNCC established several voter registration drives to raise black voting numbers across Mississippi. However, the drives were effectively shut down by white attacks and arrests by the Mississippi police force, which was widely discriminatory and corrupt.

Banding Together

In February 1962, the national civil rights groups the NAACP, SNCC, and CORE joined efforts in Mississippi

Four black college students at a whites-only lunch counter staged a nonviolent sit-in at a Greensboro, North Carolina, Woolworth's.

with the goal of addressing the state's civil rights issues. The groups would function in Mississippi under a statewide parent organization, the Council of Federated Organizations (COFO). The national branches would continue work outside the state and maintain their separate identities, but COFO would sponsor and oversee their concentrated efforts in Mississippi. This was done in part to avoid competition between groups and also to ensure everyone was working in unity.

That summer, SNCC began establishing itself in the Mississippi Delta region, where blacks made up more than half the population but most counties did not have one registered black voter. Delta native Fannie Lou Hamer, who later became an influential Freedom Summer leader, had not even realized she had the right to vote until SNCC told her in 1962.

Moses focused his efforts in the Mississippi Delta, which historians have called "the most impoverished and explosive spot in America."[7] The region lived up to its reputation in March 1963, when a voting rights drive in the Delta town of Greenwood, Mississippi, ended in chaos. To deter blacks from registering, locals engaged in drive-by shootings and torched black homes. County officials denied poor blacks federally allotted rations they needed to survive the winter. By the end of the

SIT-IN MOVEMENT AND SNCC

Black civil rights activist Ella Baker guided and encouraged the formation of the Student Nonviolent Coordinating Committee (SNCC) on April 15, 1960, in Raleigh, North Carolina, as a way to organize frequent student sit-ins.

SNCC grew and formed chapters at college campuses across the country. Members were called SNCCs, pronounced "snicks." They reinvigorated the civil rights movement with their projects and campaigns that focused on taking direct action. These tactics included sit-ins, Freedom Rides on segregated buses, and voter registration drives in Mississippi. The SNCC philosophy was to champion group efforts and celebrate success of the outcome, not the individual.

voting campaign that spring, only 13 new blacks had registered.[8]

Freedom Election

In the fall of 1963, Moses organized yet another voter campaign in Mississippi. That fall, the state would hold an election for a new governor and lieutenant governor.

SNCC and COFO decided to hold a mock election, called Freedom Election, parallel to the state's election. The plan was that disenfranchised black Mississippians across the state would participate, casting mock Freedom Ballots for one of four candidates: three black and one white. The votes collected would not be official, but organizers hoped the participation would communicate blacks' interest in voting if given the opportunity.

On November 7, thousands of black Mississippians voted in black churches, businesses, and homes across the state. White Mississippians attacked Freedom Election voters with fists, rocks, and gunfire. Local policemen confiscated many ballots, effectively hampering the Freedom Election's goals. Campaign organizers hoped 200,000 black Mississippians would cast votes in the mock election. In the end, 82,000—

less than half—actually voted.[9] However, this number did not reflect the numerous ballots taken by police.

Freedom Summer Formation

Following the Freedom Election, it was apparent a new approach—and great change—was needed. On November 11, SNCC held a meeting in Greenville, North Carolina. The idea was proposed that a massive group of activists and volunteers flood the entire state of Mississippi in a large-scale push for rights. It is unclear who first voiced the idea, but Moses is most often given credit, saying the Freedom Election made it clear to him an army was necessary to secure black Mississippians' right to vote. A professor from North Carolina, Allard Lowenstein, is also credited with inspiring the idea. Lowenstein chaperoned many college students from top colleges Stanford and Yale to

REGISTRATION LITERACY TESTS

The voter registration tests blacks had to pass often contained tricky or confusing wording. Some versions of tests were impossible to pass because answers to questions were open to interpretation. For example, blacks were often asked to read and then interpret a section of the state constitution chosen by the registrar. If the registrar was not personally satisfied with their interpretations, the voters were denied registration.

assist in the Freedom Election, and he thought bringing even more would be effective.

The proposed project would send 1,000 college students, mainly white and from the North, to Mississippi for one summer. The number of volunteers would be nearly ten times that of the efforts of the past few years, which would also allow them to address other community needs. A larger project would be harder to shut down. More workers meant more were available to directly address broader concerns in black Mississippi communities, such as the lack of education and extensive poverty. College students were made the target

ROBERT MOSES

Robert "Bob" Moses grew up in Harlem, New York. He studied at Harvard University and became a math teacher. In the 1950s, Moses became interested in the civil rights movement and began working with the Southern Christian Leadership Conference (SCLC). Moses later became involved with SNCC. In 1961, Moses moved to Mississippi and lived there for close to four years, throughout the Freedom Summer campaign

Moses became the SNCC project director in Mississippi and the COFO director. He also took part in the Freedom Rides and Freedom Election and helped establish the Mississippi Freedom Democratic Party during his lifetime.

In 1982, Moses developed the Algebra Project, which promoted math literacy. The nonprofit program focuses on using the organizing tradition and new ways of teaching to make sure students of all backgrounds in states across the nation receive adequate math skills.

volunteers because most had summer months free. Also, arrest was almost guaranteed, and most working adults would not be able to accommodate being in jail.

Organizers hoped a large number of white students giving up their summer for the cause would force the rest of the nation, which up until then had showed overwhelming indifference to black community conditions in Mississippi, to recognize that there was an urgent problem there that needed attention. Organizers of the project wagered correctly: white students' involvement effectively created national interest. That violence against blacks was largely ignored until whites spoke in defense of it—or placed themselves in danger to eradicate it—was proof of the level of racism that existed in the United States at the time. Project success in the state project organizers called "the stronghold of racial intolerance in the South" would ideally encourage and speed civil rights success in other Southern states.[10]

Politically, the project timing would coincide with the US presidential election that would occur in the fall of 1964, making it a prime time to bring discriminatory voting rights issues to the national spotlight.

Organization leaders debated the idea for months. On December 15, COFO named Moses project director for black voter registration throughout the state, but the group remained undecided about the summer project. On December 31, SNCC held an executive meeting and decided to go ahead with the campaign. If COFO did as well, the project would move forward. The new year came and went without a decision.

Freedom Day

On January 16, 1964, COFO proposed the formation of a Mississippi state Democratic Party that included blacks. Mississippi was a one-party state, meaning most Mississippi voters, nearly all white, voted for the same party. Therefore, the established party in Mississippi consisted of all-white delegates. COFO wanted to challenge the standard all-white delegation with a party that more honestly represented the Mississippi demographic by including blacks. Discussion of this idea would continue in coming months.

Days later, on January 22, in Hattiesburg, Mississippi, 150 black residents attempted to register to vote with the help of COFO.[11] The event became known as the first Freedom Day, and would be replicated in the coming year. During Freedom Days, blacks would

Robert Moses was a calm leader who played a crucial role in keeping COFO's focus on voter registration for blacks in Mississippi.

gather to register at county courthouses while picketers marched outside to show support.

On January 31, NAACP representative Louis Allen was murdered in Liberty, Mississippi, over his involvement with voter registration efforts. The tragedy helped many COFO leaders who were undecided about the summer project make up their minds. On February 9, the project was approved.

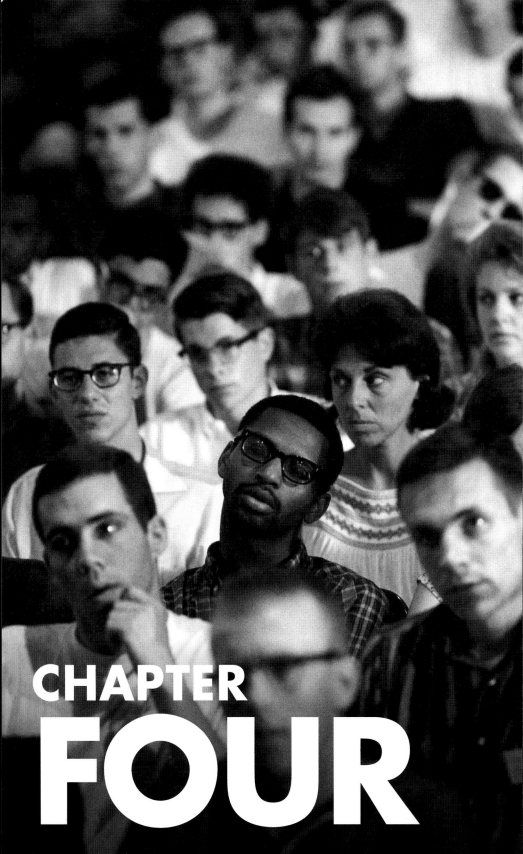

CHAPTER
FOUR

SPRING TRAINING

Once the decision to move forward with Freedom Summer was finalized, organizers defined several goals for the project. Voter registration was a main focus. In 1964, the number of black voters in Mississippi was 28,500, which was just 6.7 percent of the black population.[1] A large portion of volunteers would act as canvassers, discussing voting with disenfranchised blacks.

Freedom Summer Goals

The project aimed to erect more than 40 Freedom Schools. The schools would be makeshift, established in churches or shacks, or sometimes even outdoors. Topics would include basics such as typing and reading and extracurricular classes such as music and art. Black history, often left out in the textbooks the state provided, would also be covered, as well as politics and disenfranchisement.

Training volunteers for Freedom Summer took place in Oxford, Ohio, at the Western College for Women.

Creating Community Centers, or Freedom Houses, was another goal. These would be centers of congregation staffed by social workers, librarians, and Freedom Summer workers. The centers would provide offerings on topics ranging from hygiene, child care, and nutrition information to dance, music, and vocational training. Project offices would also serve as work bases for staff. Volunteers and staffers would stay in the homes of black citizens who volunteered to act as hosts.

Logistics and Leadership

SNCC, CORE, and COFO worked out project leadership. COFO would oversee the project, but SNCC was the unofficial leader. This was due to the group's experience in prior Mississippi campaigns

FREEDOM SUMMER FUNDING

Freedom Summer volunteers were not paid during the project. Staffers were paid a small amount, when and if funds were available. However, the project required a lot of fund-raising to stock Freedom Schools and offices with supplies, for travel funds, and for legal expenses. SNCC began fund-raising in February by publishing ads in newspapers asking for donations of money and school supplies and books. Affiliated civil rights groups across the country hosted benefits to raise money for the project. By March, $97,000 was raised.[2] But the campaign would need more, as the staffers and organizers already had gone many weeks without getting paid.

since 1961, and also because SNCC provided funding for 90 to 95 percent of the project and had the largest percentage of workers involved in Freedom Summer.[3]

Specific project sites were focused in cities and towns across five established districts. Extremely rural areas were deemed too dangerous for outposts. The southwest corner of the state, District Three, was considered the most dangerous district and was the target of two-thirds of all bombings during Freedom Summer, due to a high population of KKK in the region.

Recruiting Volunteers

Throughout March and April, SNCC members traveled to college campuses throughout the country to recruit volunteers. Some college students were shocked at the horror occurring in their own country. Many were inspired to become part of the change. COFO officially announced the Freedom Summer Project in a nationwide press release on March 30. By this time, the project had already drawn interest from many potential volunteers.

Interest was not enough to secure a spot in the campaign, however. All potential volunteers had to fill out an application and make it through an interview process to ensure they were involved for the right reasons and could comply with project rules.

The Mississippi Freedom Democratic Party

On April 26, SNCC formed the Mississippi Freedom Democratic Party (MFDP). The plan was to send the mainly black MFDP to the Democratic National Convention (DNC) held in Atlantic City, New Jersey, that coming August. There, the MFDP would challenge the all-white party that represented Mississippi and request the integrated party be seated instead. Seated parties at the DNC voted for the Democratic candidate who would run for president of the United States.

Organizers planned to have Freedom Summer workers do canvassing work to get black Mississippians to sign up as Freedom Democrats, or party supporters.

As the civil rights movement gained momentum, more blacks found the courage to register to vote.

Project organizers knew some black Mississippians would be hesitant. Registering openly took great courage. Even hosting canvassers on their front porches or in their yards could make blacks a target for white supremacists.

Moses wanted to present the list of Freedom Democrats at the DNC at the end of summer. His goal was to compile as many as 400,000 signatures, which he hoped would prove support of the party and secure them seats at the convention.[5] Before tactics to accomplish this feat were in order, organizers focused on wading through volunteers' applications.

Choosing Volunteers

By the end of May, more than 700 students had applied to volunteer during Freedom Summer.[6] Applications continued to roll in through June. By this time, the number of volunteers chosen for the project totaled 900. Of those, 135 were black.[7]

Volunteer participation was organized into one of four jobs: Freedom School teachers, voting rights workers, staff to run Freedom Houses, and those handling special projects. All volunteers would go through preparatory training before leaving for Mississippi. The first group, consisting of voting rights workers, trained between June 14 and June 20. Freedom School teachers and community center staff would train the following week, from June 22 to June 27.

Training in Ohio

On Sunday, June 14, the first group poured into the Western College for Women in Oxford, Ohio, for training. The training sessions would educate all volunteers on Mississippi culture and history, teach them how to conduct and protect themselves, including how to survive a beating, and coach them on how to achieve project goals while adhering to nonviolent tactics. Volunteers would also learn about the MFDP, its goals, and their role in supporting it.

SNCC members wanted volunteers to understand what a dangerous undertaking the campaign would be. On Monday, June 15, volunteers were told that all white institutions in the state, including law enforcement, local media, business owners, and a majority of white citizens, would be working against them. They were told these whites would use whatever tactics they could—including arson and murder—to stop Freedom Summer volunteers from achieving their goals.

PREPPING FOR THE SUMMER

Once accepted into the project, Freedom Summer volunteers were mailed letters to prepare them for the summer. The letters reminded them of the conditions in Mississippi and that they would risk arrest, injury, or death as a Freedom Summer volunteer. Arrest records might tarnish their reputations and ruin future college or career plans. Reacting to violence with nonviolence was difficult but would be expected at all times that summer.

Each volunteer was to bring $650: $150 to cover expenses such as room and board, which was eight dollars a week per student, and $500 to cover bail fees when they were inevitably jailed.[8] They were also told to bring three publicity photos of themselves and ten names of locals or media members from their hometowns that might be helpful contacts for SNCC to keep Freedom Summer in the news.

Freedom Summer volunteers were taught how to protect themselves should they encounter police brutality.

Native black Mississippians shared personal stories of being tortured in prison, attacked by police dogs, and surviving drive-by shootings inside their homes. Volunteers were warned they might endure similar scenes during the project, but they must react nonviolently no matter what. A few volunteers almost reconsidered their participation that first night, but by morning, none had gone home.

SNCC members became worried the stories had not deterred volunteers, as though they were not taking the danger seriously enough. Volunteers stayed on, but the SNCCs were right—they had reason to be scared. As they trained, white Mississippi was also preparing for their arrival.

Bracing for an Invasion

Freedom Summer leaders announced to the media several times that the project's goal was to build up Mississippi, not agitate it. Freedom Summer workers did not plan to work against the federal or Mississippi government, but simply to work for voters' rights, literacy, and improved black and white relations. However, the governor warned the "invaders" would be dealt with "Mississippi style."[9] The Jackson police force stocked up on shotguns and teargas and even brought in a six-short ton (5.4 metric ton) armored vehicle.

FREEDOM SUMMER SPIES

The impending arrival of Freedom workers prompted the Mississippi State Sovereignty Commission to employ two blacks to infiltrate Freedom Summer and act as spies. The commission publicly claimed it monitored civil rights activities in the state, but it was later discovered it had worked secretly to dismantle the civil rights movement. One of the commission's spies became a Freedom Summer worker and attended training in Ohio, reporting back to the commission on what occurred. The other became a worker at the COFO and Freedom Summer headquarters in Jackson, Mississippi. He stole important documents, such as lists of all volunteers' personal information, and sent the commission detailed reports on the project's activity.

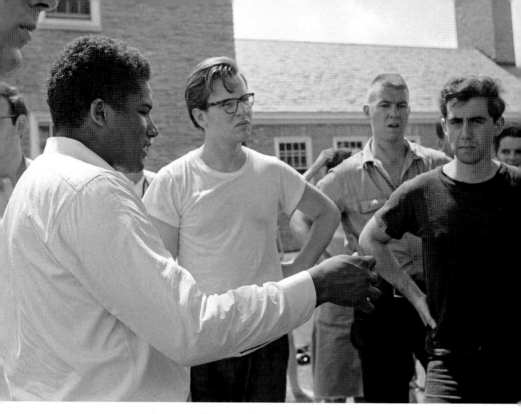

Andrew Goodman, *right*, seen here at training, was a student at Queens College in New York at the time of his murder.

Hate groups in the state stockpiled shotguns, kerosene for starting fires, and dynamite for bombing. The most vocal and active of these groups was the KKK, which prepared for an all-out "holy war." It had 91,000 members in Mississippi and was recruiting more all the time.[10]

Denied Protection

On Thursday, June 18, volunteers wrote President Lyndon B. Johnson. They requested the president speak out in support of the project and offer them federal protection. Moses had already done this, but he heard no response. The president did not respond to volunteers' pleas either.

On the evening of Friday, June 19, the Ohio campus buzzed with breaking news: the senate had passed President Johnson's civil rights bill, which demanded the entire country desegregate. As volunteers and staffers discussed this news and rested for the next day's departure, eight workers, which included CORE members Schwerner, Goodman, and Chaney, set off for Mississippi in a station wagon at 3:00 a.m. The workers left early to investigate recent news of a black church being burned in Neshoba County, Mississippi.

The next afternoon, Saturday, June 20, approximately 250 volunteers packed into buses and volunteers' cars and headed South.[11] Members of the media, who had been ever-present during training, swarmed the buses and followed volunteers and staff to Mississippi, trying to get firsthand accounts.

The first bus crossed into Mississippi at midnight. When this happened, volunteers, who up till then had spent much of the bus ride bolstering their spirits by singing freedom anthems, fell silent. Lining the highway was a chain of police cars, awaiting their arrival.

CHAPTER
FIVE

STORMING THE SOUTH

On June 21, 1964, the first day Freedom Summer workers were in Mississippi, their job was to simply settle into its black communities and get to know black citizens. After picking up the workers who would be staying at his home at the Batesville bus stop early Sunday morning, black Mississippian Robert Miles took them to his home. As members walked inside, they noticed bullet holes in Miles's modest house. Inside were guns hiding behind doors, ready to be grabbed at a moment's notice. Breakfast waited for them, cooked by Miles's wife. Freedom Workers ate heartily and learned about Miles's family and life and farm. Afterward, they attended church together.

Warm Welcome

Volunteers were prepared for the volatile reaction of white Mississippians. But they had not been prepared for

Volunteer students boarded buses and left Oxford, Ohio, with buoyed spirits, encouraging each other by singing freedom anthems.

the welcome they would receive from the black community. For many black Mississippians, these interactions were the first time they were treated with respect by whites. Black host families throughout Mississippi proudly showed their guests around town. As host Hamer recalled, these interactions were responsible for much of the change Freedom Summer incited.

During their hearty welcome, Freedom workers took in their surroundings. The poverty was shocking to many. Workers saw homes without plumbing or with raw sewage in their backyards. Some residents went without food or clothing. Lack of health care was evident.

Volunteers had been warned about night in Mississippi. They were not to go anywhere alone, but especially not at night, as darkness increased the likelihood of danger. Black hosts were immediately

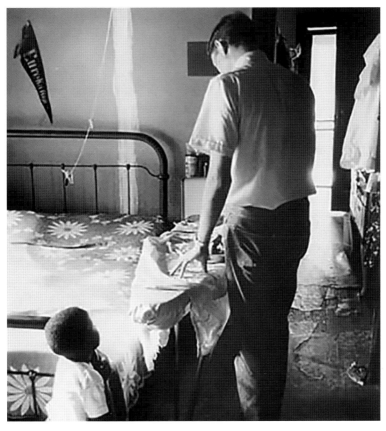
Despite grave risk, white college students lived with black host families in Mississippi during the summer of 1964 for the Freedom Summer project.

protective of their Freedom Summer guests. As night fell on June 21, 18-year-old volunteer Chris Williams witnessed Miles and his eldest son grab guns from inside the house and set up on a flatbed truck outside. They sat ready to shoot anyone who threatened them or their guests, as did many other hosts throughout that summer's nights.

White Welcome

To many Freedom Summer workers, entering the state had seemed a little "anticlimactic" after all the warnings.[2] But most had not yet heard what had already happened to three of their fellows.

Shortly after noon on June 21, after sleeping and eating upon arriving in Meridian, Schwerner, Goodman, and Chaney took off for nearby Neshoba County. The area was known for its high concentration of KKK members. They intended to investigate the church burning. The workers had a safety plan: if they were not back in four hours, by 4:00 p.m., the Meridian office was to notify headquarters and get help. The time came and went, and the trio was not back. An office worker called headquarters, but all the leaders

MISSISSIPPI: FIRST IMPRESSIONS

Volunteers' introduction to Mississippi included scorching temperatures and insects buzzing through thick, muggy air. Many experienced classic Southern foods, such as collard greens and chitlins, which were spicy pig intestines, for the first time. Volunteers witnessed people living in shacks that looked too run-down to house any human being. Porches sagged with rot, and stench wafted from old outhouses. Black children often had untreated sores on their limbs. Some were too weak from lack of food to run around the neighborhood.

were in Ohio receiving the second group of trainees. The fill-in person in charge at headquarters advised the Meridian office to hold off calling jails, which was the first step in locating missing workers.

One hour later, the men had not returned. A Meridian worker called nearby jails, but all gave the same answer: they had not arrested and were not holding the men. Night fell with no word on the missing men.

Breaking News and Rising Fear

As Freedom Summer workers woke to their first full day in Mississippi on Monday, June 22, they were still unaware three colleagues had been swallowed by the night. Staffers in Meridian had made calls into the early morning hours to the local police force, which was no help, and finally to the missing men's families.

That morning, a jailer's wife admitted she had seen the men in custody the night before at the Neshoba County jail in Philadelphia, Mississippi, but that they had been released two hours later. Local police were not talking.

The Search Begins

As news of the disappearance spread, it rattled the Freedom Summer workers beginning their first day of service in Mississippi. When the trainees in Ohio heard about the missing men, fear overtook many. For the remainder of the second group's training, the horror stories SNCC staffers had shared with the first group of volunteers no longer seemed needed. The volunteers were terrified, realizing that in one week they could be in the same situation.

The nation buzzed about the disappearance. Usually, disappearances—and possible murders—related to racial hatred were not much news in Mississippi, or across the South, for that matter. Victims of racial violence in the state were usually blacks, and the nation looked the other way. But when two white Northerners became the targets of Mississippi violence, the story immediately became a national concern. This was another example of how racism permeated American culture, media, and government at the time.

By Monday evening, US Attorney General Robert Kennedy ordered the FBI to launch an investigation. The agents received a hostile welcome from local whites,

The discovery of the charred remains of Goodman, Schwerner and Chaney's car confirmed the trio had met with foul play.

most claiming the Freedom Summer workers had staged the event to gain publicity for their project. Lawrence Rainey, sheriff of Neshoba County, was one who voiced this opinion.

On Tuesday afternoon, the station wagon the men had driven out of town was found north of Philadelphia, near the edge of a swamp. It had been burned, and it was empty. The search for the missing men would stretch for weeks, heightening tensions across the state.

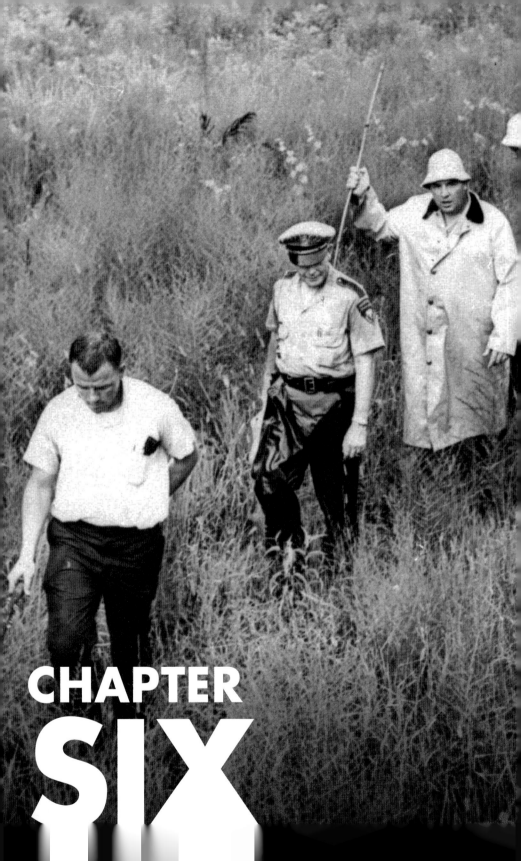

CHAPTER
SIX

EARLY SUMMER: SURVIVING IN MISSISSIPPI

By the fifth night of Freedom Summer, Schwerner, Goodman, and Chaney's disappearance had become a national obsession. White Mississippi was seething over the negative publicity and the influx of Freedom Summer workers, media, FBI agents, and search teams. Tensions rose. Mississippi exploded in waves of violence. Across the state, volunteers were harassed, chased by trucks, and arrested for fabricated reasons. A black church was lit on fire and another was threatened with a bombing.

Unlike the first group of trainees, who had been accused of not taking the Mississippi horror stories seriously enough, the second group of trainees in Ohio were becoming more terrified with every report of violence. A psychiatrist came to campus and met with

Through the blistering heat of the Deep South summer, FBI agents combed ditches and dredged lakes searching for the missing men.

frightened volunteers. He sent eight home. Some trainees retained their gusto, whether scared or not: "You know what we're all doing," one volunteer reassured the others. "We're moving the world."[1]

Into the Battle Zone

On Friday, June 26, the second group of trainees met in the auditorium at the Western College for Women. There, Moses quietly made an announcement to the crowd. "The kids are dead," he said, referring to Schwerner, Goodman, and Chaney.[2] He went on to say he had known right away they must be dead, but had not wanted to say anything in front of Schwerner's wife, Rita, who had held out hope they were alive and was now in Mississippi. Moses told the group there might be more deaths. He encouraged volunteers to weigh their decision to leave for Mississippi

Rita Schwerner, wife of slain volunteer Michael Schwerner, also attended CORE training with her husband.

the next day. He said what they were doing had to be done, but he understood if some could not go through with it. The volunteers were moved, some to tears. Some were even more inspired to join the others already entrenched in battle.

Buses and volunteers' cars holding the second round of volunteers, approximately 300, arrived in Mississippi at 2:00 p.m. on Sunday, June 28.[3] Volunteers spread to outposts throughout the state in numbers dependent on size of the planned projects. Some towns had as many as 50 volunteers, some as few as two. The early total of 550 volunteers increased, as approximately 400 to 450 volunteers joined the campaign throughout August.[4]

School Prep and Office Work

Monday morning, June 29, volunteers got to work converting the spaces that would become Freedom Schools. Books were delivered, and volunteers painted,

A TYPICAL SUMMER DAY'S WORK

A typical day of work in a Freedom Summer office consisted of handling media correspondence, answering calls, writing letters, compiling reports, and holding meetings about the project. The office was also a donation collection center for books, clothes, and supplies.

Canvassers began their typical workday that summer by looking over a map and choosing a location to target. They would drive from home to home, trying to knock on the doors of blacks only to avoid confrontation with angry whites. Blacks were usually wary when they saw white volunteers approach. But most had heard of the summer project and listened to canvassers explain voting rights and project goals. For the thousands of blacks who agreed to register, workers would either meet them at the courthouse or pick them up and drive them there themselves for support.

set up bookshelves, and cleaned. Several schools opened that Friday, July 2.

In Jackson, the Freedom Summer headquarters was bustling in full swing the first week of July. Volunteers had settled in, and the headquarters' staff were kept busy handling media and donations and keeping track of volunteers. Freedom Summer staffers knew they had to start thinking about the DNC, but in early July, their first focus was on getting canvassers to work registering as many black voters as they could. Several city-focused Freedom Days were planned in towns across the state as well, where the entire group of workers in a location would all focus their energies on getting voters registered in one-day pushes.

In the beginning, many black Mississippians were reluctant to get involved with voting efforts, afraid of whites' reactions. Although many blacks had given volunteers a warm welcome, some were completely silent and withdrawn when Freedom Summer volunteers entered their community or spoke to them. Speaking to the white volunteers at all, much less about black voting rights, could incite the rage of white Mississippians. Many blacks had to learn to trust the volunteers before they so much as spoke to them. But canvassers kept at it day after day, returning to some homes more than once. Some may have supported the project's goals internally, but they remained silent, feeling it was too risky to get involved. But many others who were formerly hesitant eventually warmed to the project and its volunteers. Eventually, disenfranchised blacks began forming lines at county courthouses around the state.

Law Enforcement Suspects and a New Law

By early July, the FBI began suspecting Neshoba County sheriff Rainey and his deputy Cecil Price had something to do with the disappearance of the three Freedom Summer workers. A highway patrolman had secretly given the FBI a list with seven men's names and told them that although he could not prove it, he believed the men he listed on the sheet were involved in the trio's disappearance. Rainey was on the list. On July 2, the FBI called the sheriff in for questioning. The KKK was an obvious suspect in the case, and it was never clear who was involved with the organization. Questioning that day did not clear up anything. Rainey did not share any information, and the FBI could not confirm his or Price's involvement.

That evening, a great advance was made supporting civil rights across the nation. At 7:00 p.m., President Johnson signed the Civil Rights Act of 1964 into law, effective immediately. Through the act, discrimination in public places, including privately owned businesses, was banned. Blacks across the nation tested out the new ruling, entering white barbershops, restaurants, and other places formerly off-limits. SNCC decided it would not push things in Mississippi by testing out the bill and integrating. And it convinced most local blacks not to either, but to wait a little longer until things had settled down.

Meanwhile, small steps of progress had also been made in some towns. In Greenville, the

CIVIL RIGHTS ACT OF 1964

In the spring of 1963, President John F. Kennedy responded to a violent scene in Birmingham, Alabama, by drafting a new civil rights bill and submitting it to Congress. The event that moved him was enacted by hundreds of black children marching over several days in early May to protest segregation. The children were met with extreme violence by the Birmingham police force, which attacked them with high-pressure water hoses, dogs, and clubs. The nation was outraged, as was the president. President Kennedy was assassinated before his bill was passed by Congress or signed into law, but his successor, Lyndon B. Johnson, continued pushing for its passing. On July 2, 1964, President Johnson signed the act into law, encouraging school desegregation and abolishing discrimination in public facilities and discriminatory hiring practices.

project held a protest over the president denying protective troops to Mississippi, but not one volunteer who marched in the protest was arrested.

On Sunday, July 5, NAACP leaders flew into Jackson to test the Civil Rights Act. They checked into a formerly whites-only hotel and ate in a formerly whites-only restaurant with no incident. To anyone unfamiliar with Mississippi's history, it might have seemed Mississippi was going to obey the new law.

Perhaps the sentiment Liz Fusco, coordinator of the CORE Freedom Schools, wrote in a project brochure would prove right: "The transformation of Mississippi is possible because the transformation of people has begun. And if it can happen in Mississippi, it can happen all over the South."[5]

Freedom Schools became a major success of Freedom Summer 1964.

But Monday, July 6, events occurred reminding workers why they were in Mississippi. Three black churches were set afire, and two in Raleigh, Mississippi, burned completely to the ground. During a civil rights meeting in Moss Point, Mississippi, a local black woman was shot by whites driving past, but only the three black men who pursued the car were arrested.

Success and tragedy, small victories and violence, continued overlapping. But one area of the project had kicked off to almost unanimous success: the Freedom Schools. Turnout was higher than expected, attitudes were positive, and change seemed within grasp immediately.

CHAPTER SEVEN

SCHOOL, POVERTY, AND POLITICS

The Mississippi weather intensified in July, shifting between scorching heat and miserably wet and heavy rains. Local temperaments reflected the turbulent weather. The first full week the Civil Rights Act of 1964 was in effect, many Mississippi businesses began shutting down to avoid integrating, including hotels, parks, libraries, and swimming pools.

By this time, most people in the nation had come to realize and accept that the three missing Freedom Summer workers were probably dead. Men had searched muddy rivers, inky black swamps, and the charred vehicle without uncovering any clues. National attention waned without fresh evidence or leads. The search continued, however, as Freedom Summer workers shifted their attention to project schools opening across the state.

Volunteer Freedom Summer teachers made do with makeshift classrooms, often resorting to holding classes outdoors for their black students.

Summer School

In 1964, Mississippi was the only Southern state that had not desegregated its schools per the *Brown v. Board of Education* decision made ten years earlier. White schools in the state received four times as much funding as black schools.[1] Black schools had few materials, old textbooks, and extremely low graduation rates. Freedom Schools sought to fill in the gaps public schools in Mississippi had created. Learning would be taken seriously at the Freedom Schools, but there would not be any tests or homework, and attendance was voluntary.

Turnout was overwhelming at nearly all locations. Freedom Summer organizers originally hoped to enroll approximately 1,000 students in Freedom Schools. More than 35 Freedom Schools were established by mid-July, with approximately 2,100 daily student attendees across the state.[2] Interested students were drawn from a much wider age range than organizers originally expected. Attendees ranged anywhere from preschool-age children to senior citizens. In most places, attendance was so much higher than expected that schools had to hold classes morning, afternoon, and evening to accommodate. They also had to bring in more teachers to many outposts.

Teachers across the state were pleasantly surprised with students' universal eagerness to learn. They were also shocked at how little some knew about the basics and black history. In Greenwood, a student named Endesha Ida Mae Holland was surprised to learn there were black authors. "I'd always been told blacks had done no great things, they hadn't done anything, we had *nothing* that we could be proud of," she said.[3]

In addition to basics such as reading and math and extracurricular music or art classes, students were taught leadership skills that would allow them to continue fighting for civil rights beyond that summer. Teachers encouraged black students' abilities and interests in questioning their current situation in Mississippi. As the SNCC teaching guidebook explained to teachers:

"To think of kids in Mississippi . . . being willing to come to school after school, day *after* day, when their whole association with school has been at best uncomfortable and dull and at worst tragically crippling—to think of these things is to think that a total transformation of these young people can take place, and to dare to dream that [it] can happen all over the South."[4]
— Liz Fusco, Coordinator of CORE Freedom Schools

You will be teaching young people who have lived in Mississippi all their lives. That means that they have been deprived of decent education from first grade through high school. It means that they have been denied free expression and free thought. Most of all it means that they have been denied the right to question. The purpose of Freedom Schools is to help them begin to question.[5]

In Clarksdale, Mississippi, one teacher told black students that she believed the oppression happening to them was criminal. With encouragement such as this, students slowly began opening up and questioning discrimination they had faced.

Anger and Exhaustion

In mid-July, some Freedom Summer workers were getting frustrated their efforts had not had much impact on racial violence in Mississippi. Some were upset to learn the horror stories they had been told in training had proved so true. Others grew angry the federal government had never stepped in to help Mississippi before and still would not.

On July 16, a Freedom Day was planned in locations across the state. In Greenwood, police were present and trouble was expected. But workers were surprised when

Citizens remembered the three murdered civil rights workers during a memorial march through Philadelphia, Mississippi, on June 21, 1965.

the only ones arrested that day were the picketers, as Mississippi had enacted a new antipicketing law. Blacks, who a little more than one year ago were attacked for trying to register, were left alone. But in another overlap of triumph and tragedy, the picketers were subjected to extreme violence by police in Greenwood that day. In addition to picketers being dragged and roughed up, SNCC member Stokely Carmichael was struck with a cattle prod, which greatly tested his resolve to respond with nonviolence.

A Freedom Day was held that day in Greenville as well. There, 100 blacks filled out registration forms, but even picketers were not arrested.[6] The real progress was seen in Cleveland, Mississippi, that day: not only did more than two dozen blacks fill out registration forms and picketers escape arrest, but cops held back angry whites from attacking.[7]

Collectively, white segregationists in Mississippi were displeased with these advances, as well as with the recent national advances made by law. Across the nation, whites were angry at blacks for gaining their rights. They feared blacks would take white jobs, and that black men would start dating white women.

Even white citizens across the United States who publicly claimed they backed integration proved hesitant to actually let it happen. A poll revealed more than two-thirds of Americans opposed the summer project in Mississippi.[8] Many were upset so much national attention and resources had been sourced to the project, especially concerning the search for the trio of missing workers. A Louisiana resident asked: "By what stretch of the imagination does anyone consider that these kids have any right in Mississippi in the first place? The whole situation is disgusting."[10]

Other US citizens, however, were disgusted Mississippi was a part of their country due to recent events including the disappearance of three Freedom Summer workers. Some wondered aloud if there was a way to force certain Southern states to secede, as they had done during the Civil War. White US citizens who admired Freedom Summer workers spoke of their strength and courage. There were even whites in Mississippi who supported the project, although usually quietly. In Hattiesburg, workers witnessed whites secretly donating money and food to the project efforts.

Taking Stock and Inspiring Endurance

By the third week of July, many volunteers had gone home out of fear. Some who stayed were becoming numb to the violence. One volunteer wrote home to his parents describing violent scenes and then added, "Ho hum. This violent life rolls on. We Shall Overcome."[11]

However, reducing this extreme violence to a flippant remark may have been some volunteers' way of mentally dealing with the hostile environment. The movement was gaining momentum, and workers were becoming bolder. Volunteers began flooding towns formerly thought too dangerous to integrate. COFO sued Rainey, the KKK, and the White Citizens Council for widespread acts of terror against blacks. No one truly expected COFO to win the suits, but just the fact they were filed signaled a shift in atmosphere.

In late July, leaders tried to determine what they had accomplished so far. Freedom Schools were a great success, with massive enrollment and eager participants. Voter registration, however, was at a bit of a standstill. In Canton, Mississippi, 22 blacks had applied to register, but all had failed registration tests. In Hattiesburg, 70 applied, but just five passed. In Greenwood, 123 applied, but just two were successfully registered.[12] Freedom Summer organizers decided to shift their focus on MFDP support into high gear.

Workers flooded black places of congregation with campaign announcements. They took out radio and newspaper ads. Workers convinced blacks that signing the paper making them Freedom Democrat supporters was safe. Their names would not be published anywhere, and no one would know they did it. But some were still hesitant, so Freedom workers showed up time and again, explaining and urging them to sign.

In late July, Martin Luther King Jr. arrived to tour the state in promotion of the project and the party. Between July 21 and 25, King, who believed Freedom Summer was "the most creative thing happening today in civil rights,"[13] met black Mississippians and gave inspiring speeches in support of the MFDP. He urged black Mississippians to sign up as Freedom Democrats and continue fighting for the right to vote, effectively

FREEDOM SUMMER VISITORS

King was not the only outside participant in Freedom Summer. Doctors and nurses from across the country visited Mississippi for weeks at a time, aiding volunteers and blacks with health issues. Lawyers also came periodically to help out with lawsuits. Other celebrities visited during the project as well. Actress Shirley MacLaine, Celtics basketball star Bill Russell, and several popular folk singers also made their way to Mississippi to meet volunteers and black Mississippians and show them support.

King's visit was a concern for the federal government, as there had been rumors swirling that white Mississippians were plotting to kill him during his tour. King wanted to go despite the risk and made it safely through his tour, which included stops in Jackson, Vicksburg, Philadelphia, and Meridian.

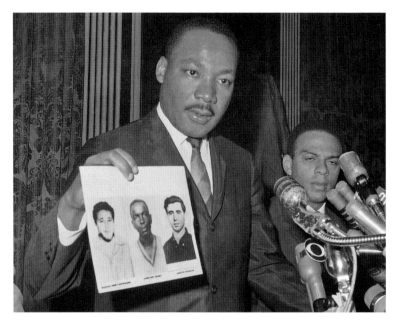

Martin Luther King Jr. gained media attention when he toured Mississippi in late July, encouraging blacks to sign up as Freedom Democrats.

swaying some hesitant people to become involved. Although he inspired local black Mississippians, several SNCC members were less enthusiastic about his visit. Many sarcastically referred to King as "de Lawd"[14] behind his back and resented the media attention he received for his brief involvement.

New Lead

By the weekend King departed Mississippi, the trio of Freedom Summer workers had been missing for five weeks. Agents still had not learned any more about their disappearance. On Friday, July 31, the FBI spoke to Rainey and Price separately, trying to make a deal with each for information about Schwerner, Goodman, and Chaney. Neither complied.

But someone talked that day. A secret informant told the FBI where the bodies were.

The next day, August 1, agents discovered the dam the informant had told them to search. The Neshoba County dam was a pile of earth approximately 20 feet (6 m) high in the center, and stretching almost the length of two football fields. The agents ordered heavy equipment for the search. Two days later, a steam shovel and bulldozer arrived, and agents began digging.

SECRET INFORMANT

Agents revealed that a secret informant had shared information about the location of Schwerner, Goodman, and Chaney's bodies before they began digging, in hopes those responsible would become scared and speak up. Speculation swirled on who the informant was and what he or she might have said. Many rumored it was a highway patrolman. There has also been longtime speculation that agents were offering a large sum of money for successful information, but this has never been confirmed. Agents kept the informant's identity secret until 2005. When his identity was revealed, it turned out suspicions had been correct: the informant was a Meridian highway patrolman who had been told the information by a KKK member.

CHAPTER
EIGHT

SEASON OF CHANGE

T he dig for the three missing civil rights workers who disappeared the first day of Freedom Summer signaled the beginning of the end of the project. As Freedom Summer drew to a close, the nation would finally have answers about what happened to the missing trio of workers, and the MFDP would challenge the white delegation at the DNC. Freedom Summer participants and black Mississippians would reflect on the summer and realize their lives, and the nation, were changed forever.

The Search Ends

The morning of August 4, 1964, FBI agents arrived at the Neshoba County dam to follow the lead that Schwerner, Goodman, and Chaney lay somewhere within the massive mound of dirt. After digging for many hours, around 5:00 p.m. agents unearthed

Fannie Lou Hamer attended the National Democratic Convention in 1964, serving as the vice-chair of the Mississippi Freedom Democratic Party.

Schwerner first. Minutes later, agents pulled Goodman from beside him. In one hand, Goodman was gripping a chunk of earth. To agents, this indicated he might have been buried injured, but alive. Chaney was pulled out next. Within hours, the news spread around the country.

Seeking Justice

As news spread, some white Mississippians began voicing new opinions about the murderers, calling for

MURDERS UNRAVELED

As Schwerner, Goodman, and Chaney's murderers came under investigation, details of the volunteers' disappearance and deaths were revealed. Schwerner had become a KKK target when he moved to Mississippi in the spring of 1964 because of his work with CORE. Chaney, also a CORE member, was targeted for his work setting up a Freedom Summer school at the Mount Zion Baptist Church in Neshoba County—the burned church the two men and fellow Freedom Summer worker Goodman investigated on June 21. Upon leaving the church, the workers were stopped by local police and arrested. They were held at the jail while the KKK formed a plan to kill them. At 10:00 p.m. that night, Deputy Price released the men, who began driving toward Meridian from the Philadelphia jail. Two cars full of KKK members chased and caught the youth and drove them to the remote Neshoba County dam. There, the men were shot at close range. Chaney, however, was first tortured and badly beaten before being shot.

justice. But many stuck to their belief the three Freedom Summer workers got what was coming to them. The confirmed deaths of the Freedom Summer workers incited anger across the country. Some SNCC members were becoming fed up with reacting nonviolently to violent attacks.

On October 13, the FBI arrested 18 male KKK members, including Rainey and Price, for involvement in the crime. Two members gave full confessions, confirming the others' involvement in the murders. Both also cited Edgar Ray "Preacher" Killen as a main coordinator of the crimes. Despite this, state prosecutors refused to try the case, stating there was a lack of evidence, and the men were released. The federal government stepped in, and the men were rearrested on December 4.

Legal proceedings stretched on. On October 2, 1967, seven of the 18 charged men were found guilty. Price was one of them, but Rainey was acquitted. The jury remained undecided about Killen. The case was reopened in 1999 after one imprisoned member supplied new evidence implicating Killen. On January 7, 2005, more than 40 years after the crime, the 80-year-old

Charges were initially dismissed against Price, *left*, Rainey, *right*, and 17 others.

was charged and sentenced to 60 years for the three murders.

Challenge at the Convention

As August 1964 continued, many volunteers were growing ready for summer's end, missing their homes and old way of life. But workers gathered their resolve for Freedom Summer's final goal. On August 6, the MFDP elected 67 delegates to represent the party at the DNC. SNCC worked overtime to promote the party, making calls, creating brochures, and canvassing for signatures.

On August 19, the MFDP delegates—64 black and four white—boarded buses for Atlantic City.[1] They brought along 63,000 Freedom Democrat signatures.[2] President Johnson, who wanted to run for another term as president, began worrying about the Freedom Democrats. He knew if the mainly black MFDP was seated it might cause the 15 other all-white parties from Southern states to walk out. The white parties backed President Johnson, and he needed their support to run for a second term.

On the first day of the convention, August 22, delegate Hamer gave a speech in front of the rules committee about life in her home state and what the MFDP meant to black Mississippians. As Hamer began speaking, her speech was aired on national television. Then, suddenly, the networks cut to an image of President Johnson. He had staged an impromptu press conference in order to prevent the nation from hearing Hamer's speech. Johnson knew Hamer's speech would likely incite citizens to call for the seating of the MFDP. He spoke about nothing of particular importance and ended just as Hamer finished her speech. However, that evening, three national networks broadcast her stirring speech across the nation in its entirety. Afterward, more than 400 telegrams were sent to the White House, and all but one demanded the MFDP be seated. The letters were unsuccessful.

The 68 MFDP delegates were offered two at-large seats as "guests" of the main delegation party, along with the stipulation that all future DNCs would ban any state delegation that discriminated against blacks. Hamer expressed the group's collective anger at the offer: "We didn't come all this way for no two seats!"[3] The MFDP refused and headed back to Mississippi. This offer and the tactics of President Johnson during the convention caused Moses and many other SNCCs never to trust politics again.

The End of Summer

As Freedom Summer drew to a close, 80 volunteers decided to stay in Mississippi indefinitely. But this was not enough to comfort many blacks who feared whites would punish them for Freedom Summer after workers departed. "If you people leave us, they are going to kill us all. They gonna pile our bodies on top of one another," one black woman claimed.[5]

After the bulk of Freedom Summer workers dispersed the third week in August, white Mississippi was left collectively shell shocked and upset about events that had made a spectacle of their state. In September, six churches were burned across the state. The KKK bombed the Natchez mayor's home and a Freedom House in Vicksburg and terrorized residents of McComb with bombs and beatings. Freedom Summer organizers struggled to measure the project's success despite the violence.

The results of Freedom Summer were an overlap of great successes and upsetting blows. Approximately

17,000 blacks attempted voter registration. However, just 1,600 passed registrars' tests and became voters.[6]

In some Mississippi towns, such as Batesville, blacks continued registering on their own after Freedom Summer workers left. Additionally, it seemed some registrars there were even helping the blacks register, afraid of being charged with discrimination if they did not.

The MFDP did not achieve its goal of being seated. However, future DNCs never again seated all-white parties for any state.

Freedom Summer had also effectively influenced the creation of a new law. President Johnson signed the Voting Rights Act of 1965 into law on August 6, 1965, which made unfair voting practices, including literacy tests, illegal across the nation. The federal government also took over voter registration in regions that had displayed proven discrimination. The new law effectively increased black voting numbers across the South, including in Mississippi, where the number of registered black voters increased from 22,000 to 150,000.[7]

Measuring whether violence decreased was more difficult. The threats, beatings, and attacks had been countless. Thirteen Mississippi citizens had been murdered that summer by unknown, or at least uncharged, attackers. Four Freedom Summer workers had died. More then 60 churches, businesses, and homes were burned or bombed, and more than 1,000 arrests were made during Freedom Summer.[8] However, it seemed violence directly aimed at blacks for attempting to register had generally waned as a result of the project.

RECENT CHANGES

On June 25, 2013, another Supreme Court case struck down a key aspect of the Voting Rights Act in nine US states: Alabama, Alaska, Arizona, Georgia, Louisiana, Mississippi, South Carolina, Texas, and Virginia. No longer would states need federal approval before changing their election laws. Several government officials were disappointed in the decision, which felt to many like a reverse step.

Freedom Schools were a more clear success. By the end of summer, more than 3,000 students attended 41 established Freedom Schools across the state, and programs continued during the school year.[9] One Freedom Summer worker, Tom Levin, developed the Child Development Group of Mississippi (CDGM) in 1965. It provided poor preschool children in Mississippi with meals, medical care, and training for school. The program grew to include branches across the nation, today known as Head Start Schools.

SNCC Shift

As historians have examined Freedom Summer in the decades since, most have determined the project overall was successful, largely due to its influence on the Voting Rights Act and Head Start Schools. However, at the time, some SNCCs felt Freedom Summer tactics had failed to produce results.

Many SNCCs became frustrated with the continued discrimination in Mississippi. When the MFDP was

INFLUENCE ON VOLUNTEERS

After Freedom Summer, many volunteers could not get Mississippi out of their minds. Some felt their life outside Mississippi was pointless when there was greater struggle going on. Some felt guilty for leaving.

Freedom Summer volunteer Ellen Lake wrote to her parents about the link between what was happening in Mississippi and the ongoing Vietnam War (1954–1975). She wrote,

> For the first time in my life, I am seeing what it's like to be poor, oppressed, and hated. And what I

see here does not only apply to Gulfport or to Mississippi, or even the South. . . . The people we're killing in Vietnam are the same people whom we've been killing for years in Mississippi. . . . We didn't pull the trigger... but we've been standing behind the . . . trigger-pullers for too long."[10]

Many shared this new outlook and questioned politics for the rest of their lives. In the years following, many volunteers were among the leading activists of the protests of the 1960s.

denied being fully seated, some members became fed up with current civil rights efforts.

Many SNCCs grew bitter against whites, even fellow members who had worked beside them. The Black Power movement, which emphasized black pride and self-determination, was growing in popularity across the nation. It centered on the idea of black individuals taking control of their own lives and communities by demanding equality through any means necessary, including self-defense. The ideology of the new movement interested many SNCC members who were frustrated with what they felt was little progress through nonviolent tactics.

SNCC members split. One camp included the few who adhered to the older, more conservative values, such as Moses. The majority of members began identifying with more aggressive tactics, including SNCC member Carmichael, who became a leader of the Black Power movement. The momentum COFO had experienced during the summer faded, and the umbrella organization dissolved. In an act characteristic of the Black Power movement, SNCC called for all whites to leave the organization. The MFDP also transformed to support the more militant movement.

Mississippi after Freedom Summer

White supremacists in Mississippi reacted to the close of Freedom Summer with outbursts of violence, just as many black Mississippians had feared. The KKK terrorized many cities with violence, church burnings, and open rallies. Mississippi again stood at a sort of crossroads, poised between new laws and old customs that died hard. Many supremacists or racists in Mississippi held on to their beliefs. But some who had been less steadfast, or who had silently opposed white supremacy, came forward as activists or supporters. Some white Mississippians may have changed because they were outnumbered or felt pressured by the national shift toward equality. Whether defeatist or sincere, these shifting attitudes in white Mississippi resulted in slow change.

In the decade that followed Freedom Summer, everyday citizens continued organizing work for equal rights. A subtle shift in the social environment was evident, even though racism had not waned significantly. As author Watson described, even "white and black slowly came together. Most found that, in hailing from that unique place called Mississippi, they had something in common. . . . Each act of kindness, each common concern helped southern hospitality melt age-old hostilities."[11]

Civil rights took hold in new parts of Mississippi as a direct result from Freedom Summer. By the end of 1964, the political climate of Mississippi included blacks and had become more centered on activism and civil rights. As SNCC chairman John Lewis correctly predicted one year after the project, "Mississippi will never be the same again, for people are in motion now."[12]

During major state elections held in 1967 and 1968, black Mississippians voted the most black officials into office since the 1800s. Freedom Summer also inspired blacks across the nation. The creation of the MFDP and collective banding

FREEDOM SUMMER REUNIONS

Many Freedom Summer workers made lifelong connections in Mississippi. Friendships were forged between people who shared the same ideologies and passions. Several participants met their future partners during the summer as well. Three years after Freedom Summer's end, there had been 31 marriages between Freedom Summer veterans, some interracial.

Thirty years later, in 1994, Freedom Summer volunteers and locals met for reunions throughout Mississippi to reminisce about the summer that changed most of their lives. Another smaller reunion was held for project veterans specifically from Hattiesburg in June 1999 at the University of Southern Mississippi.

together to fight for rights showed black US citizens they could rise up and gain political power and equality.

Personal Liberation

In the wake of political change, arguably the most important impact Freedom Summer had was on black Mississippians' way of life and sense of self. Before the project, black Mississippians collectively lacked rights, were afraid to question discrimination, were terrorized into living under extremely poor conditions, and were the victims of constant harassment, injury, and murder. By the end of summer, Mississippi blacks' confidence had risen, and they had slowly begun establishing their right to vote. Black children learned a sense of pride in their history and personhood. Black youth and adults sought leadership roles and questioned discrimination. Locals continued strengthening their social, political, and economic power. To stand on

Mount Zion Church in Neshoba County was rebuilt in 1965 after being burnt. A historic marker honors Schwerner, Goodman, and Chaney, who were killed while going to investigate the church fire.

their own and continue their fight for equality when Freedom Summer ended was perhaps the summer's most inspirational impact. As one Freedom Summer veteran later recalled, "The memories of that summer remind me . . . that people are capable of quite remarkable things."[14]

TIMELINE

Mid-1950s
The black civil rights movement begins across the United States, centered in the South.

1955
Fourteen-year-old Emmett Till is murdered in Money, Mississippi, on August 24.

1960
The Student Nonviolent Coordinating Committee (SNCC) forms.

1962
The Council of Federated Organizations (COFO) is established in February to oversee national groups' combined civil rights efforts in Mississippi.

1964
COFO announces the Freedom Summer project in a nationwide press release on March 30.

1964

On April 26, the biracial Mississippi Freedom Democratic Party (MFDP) forms.

1964

Hundreds of volunteers train for Freedom Summer at the Western College for Women in Oxford, Ohio, from June 14 to 20.

1964

On June 21, the first group of Freedom Summer workers floods Mississippi. That afternoon, Michael "Mickey" Schwerner, Andrew Goodman, and James "JE" Chaney disappear while investigating a church burning.

1964

The second group of Freedom Summer trainees arrives in Mississippi on June 28.

1964

On July 2, several Freedom Schools open across Mississippi to great success.

1964

President Lyndon B. Johnson signs the Civil Rights Act of 1964 into law on July 2, banning discrimination in public places.

TIMELINE

1964

On July 31, a secret informant reveals to the Federal Bureau of Investigation (FBI) where the bodies of the three missing Freedom Summer workers are buried.

1964

FBI agents unearth the bodies of Schwerner, Goodman, and Chaney on August 4.

1964

On August 19, MFDP delegates leave Mississippi for the Democratic National Convention (DNC) in Atlantic City, New Jersey, to challenge the all-white party that is seated.

1964

In lieu of seating the entire MFDP, DNC committees offer the MFDP delegates two "guest" seats with the current all-white party. The MFDP turns down the offer and returns to Mississippi.

1964

The majority of Freedom Summer workers leave Mississippi by the third week of August, but 80 stay indefinitely to continue civil rights work in the state.

1964

On October 13, the FBI arrests 18 Ku Klux Klan (KKK) members for the murders of Schwerner, Goodman, and Chaney. They are released when the state claims to lack evidence to convict them.

1964

The federal government orders the 18 KKK members suspected of killing the three Freedom Summer workers be rearrested on December 4.

1965

The proposed Voting Rights Act of 1965 is signed into law on August 6, banning unfair voting practices nationwide.

1967

Seven of the 18 men on trial for the murders of Schwerner, Goodman, and Chaney are found guilty and given prison sentences.

2005

On January 7, Edgar Ray "Preacher" Killen, is sentenced to prison after new information is revealed about his involvement in the Freedom Summer murders.

ESSENTIAL FACTS

Date of Event
June–August 1964

Place of Event
Mississippi

Key Players
- Robert "Bob" Moses, the director of the Student Nonviolent Coordinating Committee (SNCC) and the Coalition of Federated Organizations

- Fannie Lou Hamer and Stokely Carmichael, SNCC leaders

- Lawrence Rainey, sheriff of Neshoba County

- Nine hundred Freedom Summer volunteers

Highlights of Event
- The 1964 summer began with the disappearance of three Freedom Summer workers the first night of the project, June 21. The search for Michael "Mickey" Schwerner, Andrew Goodman, and James "JE" Chaney lasted almost the entire duration of the Freedom Summer project, and it was the subject of intense media and political scrutiny.

- On July 2, the Civil Rights Act of 1964 was signed into law, banning discrimination in public places.

- The discovery of the bodies of the three missing Freedom Summer workers on August 4 signaled the decline of the summer project.

- The third week of August, the Mississippi Freedom Democratic Party (MFDP) attended the Democratic National Convention in Atlantic City, New Jersey. The MFDP tried to get seated at the convention as Mississippi's party to vote on which democratic candidate would run for president but was denied a full seating, being offered only two seats.

- On August 6, 1965, approximately one year after Freedom Summer ended, the Voting Rights Act of 1965 was signed into law. The law, which gained momentum from Freedom Summer events, made it illegal to enact unfair voting processes, such as the literacy tests that had kept blacks in Mississippi and across the South disenfranchised for decades.

Quote

"Mississippi stood at a crossroads. Years of peaceful protest had been met with bombings, beatings, and simple murder. And the rest of America did not seem to care. . . . What if, instead of Mississippi struggling in isolation, hundreds of college students from all across the country poured into the state? Wouldn't America pay attention then?" —*author Bruce Watson, on the ideas that led to Freedom Summer*

GLOSSARY

activist
A person involved in protests, demonstrations, or campaigns in order to support social change.

assassinate
To murder an important person, such as a celebrity or government official.

canvass
To travel through a particular district or region seeking to gain political support for a project, party, or candidate through discussion.

discrimination
Unfair treatment based on a person's religion, race, or sex.

disenfranchise
To take away a person's right to vote.

ideology
A system of beliefs held by a person or group.

illiteracy
The inability to read or write.

integration
The act of mixing together different groups of people as equals.

militant
Aggressive or combative.

segregation
The act of separating groups of people based on race, religion, or other traits.

white supremacist
A person who believes white people are better than people of other races.

ADDITIONAL RESOURCES

Selected Bibliography

Bauerlein, Mark, et al. *Civil Rights Chronicle: The African-American Struggle for Freedom*. Lincolnwood, IL: Legacy, 2003. Print.

Randall, Herbert, and Bobs M. Tusa. *Faces of Freedom Summer*. Tuscaloosa: U of Alabama P, 2001. Print.

Watson, Bruce. *Freedom Summer: The Savage Season That Made Mississippi Burn and Made America a Democracy*. New York: Viking, 2010. Print.

Further Readings

Buckley, A. M. *Racism*. Minneapolis, MN: ABDO, 2011. Print.

Capek, Michael. *Civil Rights Movement*. Minneapolis, MN: ABDO, 2013. Print.

McWhorter, Diane, with foreword by Fred Shuttlesworth. *A Dream of Freedom: The Civil Rights Movement from 1954 to 1968*. New York: Scholastic, 2004. Print.

Web Sites

To learn more about the 1964 Freedom Summer, visit ABDO Publishing Company online at **www.abdopublishing.com**. Web sites about the 1964 Freedom Summer are featured on our Book Links page. These links are routinely monitored and updated to provide the most current information available.

Places to Visit

Freedom Summer Memorial
Adjacent to Kumler Chapel on Western Drive
Western College at Miami University
501 East High Street
Oxford, OH 45056
513-529-1809
http://miamioh.edu
This outdoor amphitheater was erected in 2000 to commemorate the involvement of Western Women's College, which has since merged with Miami University, during Freedom Summer training. The exhibit also memorializes the three workers who were murdered during the summer project.

Freedom Summer Trail
Five Convention Center Plaza
Hattiesburg Visitors Center
Hattiesburg, MS 39401
601-296-7475
http://www.hattiesburg.org/index.cfm/play/all-play/
freedom-summer-trail
Drive a trail linking 16 historic Freedom Summer landmarks in the Hattiesburg, Mississippi, outpost. The trail contains permanent educational markers and begins from Hattiesburg's Visitors Center, where maps and audio guides are available for tour direction and narrative.

SOURCE NOTES

Chapter 1. Summer Victims
1. Bruce Watson. *Freedom Summer: The Savage Season That Made Mississippi Burn and Made America a Democracy*. New York: Viking, 2010. Print. 9.

2. Charles M. Payne. *I've Got the Light of Freedom: The Organizing Tradition and the Mississippi Freedom Struggle*. Berkeley, CA: Berkeley UP, 1995. *Google Book Search*. Web. 14 Aug. 2013.

3. Bruce Watson. *Freedom Summer: The Savage Season That Made Mississippi Burn and Made America a Democracy*. New York: Viking, 2010. Print. 11.

Chapter 2. From Slavery to Civil Rights
1. Mark Bauerlein, et al. *Civil Rights Chronicle: The African-American Struggle for Freedom*. Lincolnwood, IL: Legacy, 2003. Print. 96.

2. "Timeline of Events Leading to the *Brown v. Board of Education* Decision, 1954." *Teachers' Resources*. National Archives, n.d. Web. 21 July 2013.

3. Bruce Watson. *Freedom Summer: The Savage Season That Made Mississippi Burn and Made America a Democracy*. New York: Viking, 2010. Print. 48.

4. Ibid.

5. Charles M. Payne. *I've Got the Light of Freedom: The Organizing Tradition and the Mississippi Freedom Struggle*. Berkeley, CA: Berkeley UP, 1995. *Google Book Search*. Web. 14 Aug. 2013.

Chapter 3. Targeting Mississippi
1. Doug McAdam. *Freedom Summer*. New York: Oxford UP, 1988. *Google Book Search*. Web. 21 July 2013.

2. Bruce Watson. *Freedom Summer: The Savage Season That Made Mississippi Burn and Made America a Democracy*. New York: Viking, 2010. Print. 10.

3. Doug McAdam. *Freedom Summer*. New York: Oxford UP, 1988. *Google Book Search*. Web. 21 July 2013.

4. Ibid.

5. Ibid.

6. Ibid.

7. Bruce Watson. *Freedom Summer: The Savage Season That Made Mississippi Burn and Made America a Democracy*. New York: Viking, 2010. Print. 49.

8. Ibid. 10–11.

9. Ibid. 8.

10. "Information Sheet: Project Mississippi; Undated." *The University of Southern Mississippi Civil Right Digital Library: Freedom Summer.* The University of Southern Mississippi, n.d. Web. 21 July 2013.

11. Herbert Randall and Bobs M. Tusa. *Faces of Freedom Summer.* Tuscaloosa: U of Alabama P, 2001. Print. 10.

Chapter 4. Spring Training

1. Chris Danielson. *After Freedom Summer: How Race Realigned Mississippi Politics, 1965–1986.* Gainesville, FL: UP of Florida, 2011. *Amazon Book Search.* Web. 23 July 2013.

2. Bruce Watson. *Freedom Summer: The Savage Season That Made Mississippi Burn and Made America a Democracy.* New York: Viking, 2010. Print. 67.

3. Doug McAdam. *Freedom Summer.* New York: Oxford UP, 1988. *Google Book Search.* Web. 21 July 2013.

4. Bruce Watson. *Freedom Summer: The Savage Season That Made Mississippi Burn and Made America a Democracy.* New York: Viking, 2010. Print. 19.

5. Ibid. 66.

6. Ibid. 18.

7. Herbert Randall and Bobs M. Tusa. *Faces of Freedom Summer.* Tuscaloosa: U of Alabama P, 2001. Print. 9.

8. Bruce Watson. *Freedom Summer: The Savage Season That Made Mississippi Burn and Made America a Democracy.* New York: Viking, 2010. Print. 19.

9. Ibid. 12.

10. Ibid. 54.

11. Doug McAdam. *Freedom Summer.* New York: Oxford UP, 1988. *Google Book Search.* Web. 21 July 2013.

Chapter 5. Storming the South

1. Bruce Watson. *Freedom Summer: The Savage Season That Made Mississippi Burn and Made America a Democracy.* New York: Viking, 2010. Print. 109.

2. Doug McAdam. *Freedom Summer.* New York: Oxford UP, 1988. *Amazon Book Search.* Web. 21 July 2013.

SOURCE NOTES CONTINUED

Chapter 6. Early Summer: Surviving in Mississippi

1. Doug McAdam. *Freedom Summer.* New York: Oxford UP, 1988. *Google Book Search.* Web. 21 July 2013.

2. Bruce Watson. *Freedom Summer: The Savage Season That Made Mississippi Burn and Made America a Democracy.* New York: Viking, 2010. Print. 101.

3. Doug McAdam. *Freedom Summer.* New York: Oxford UP, 1988. *Amazon Book Search.* Web. 21 July 2013.

4. Ibid.

5. "CORE Freedom School Brochure; Undated." *The University of Southern Mississippi Civil Right Digital Library: Freedom Summer.* The University of Southern Mississippi, n.d. Web. 21 July 2013.

Chapter 7. School, Poverty, and Politics

1. Bruce Watson. *Freedom Summer: The Savage Season That Made Mississippi Burn and Made America a Democracy.* New York: Viking, 2010. Print. 137.

2. "Mississippi Freedom Project Pamphlet; Undated." *The University of Southern Mississippi Civil Right Digital Library: Freedom Summer.* The University of Southern Mississippi, n.d. Web. 21 July 2013.

3. Bruce Watson. *Freedom Summer: The Savage Season That Made Mississippi Burn and Made America a Democracy.* New York: Viking, 2010. Print. 141.

4. "CORE Freedom School Brochure; Undated." "Mississippi Freedom Project Pamphlet; Undated." *The University of Southern Mississippi Civil Right Digital Library: Freedom Summer.* The University of Southern Mississippi, n.d. Web. 21 July 2013.

5. Bruce Watson. *Freedom Summer: The Savage Season That Made Mississippi Burn and Made America a Democracy.* New York: Viking, 2010. Print. 137.

6. Ibid. 160–161.

7. Ibid.

8. Ibid. 158.

9. "Mississippi Summer Project One Year Later; May 31, 1965." *The University of Southern Mississippi Civil Right Digital Library: Freedom Summer.* The University of Southern Mississippi, n.d. Web. 21 July 2013.

10. Bruce Watson. *Freedom Summer: The Savage Season That Made Mississippi Burn and Made America a Democracy.* New York: Viking, 2010. Print. 159.

11. Ibid. 171.

12. Ibid. 173–174.

13. Ibid. 181–182.

14. Ibid. 181.

Chapter 8. Season of Change

1. Bruce Watson. *Freedom Summer: The Savage Season That Made Mississippi Burn and Made America a Democracy.* New York: Viking, 2010. Print. 237.

2. Ibid. 243.

3. Herbert Randall and Bobs M. Tusa. *Faces of Freedom Summer.* Tuscaloosa: U of Alabama P, 2001. Print. 23.

4. Bruce Watson. *Freedom Summer: The Savage Season That Made Mississippi Burn and Made America a Democracy.* New York: Viking, 2010. Print. 249.

5. Ibid. 245.

6. "Freedom Summer (1964)." *Martin Luther King Jr. and the Global Freedom Struggle.* The Martin Luther King Jr. Research and Education Institute, Stanford University, n.d. Web. 20 July 2013.

7. Frederic O. Sargent. *The Civil Rights Revolution: Events and Leaders, 1955–1968.* Jefferson, NC: McFarland, 2004. Web. *Google Book Search.* 22 July 2013.

8. Mark Bauerlein et al. *Civil Rights Chronicle: The African-American Struggle for Freedom.* Lincolnwood, IL: Legacy, 2003. Print. 266.

9. "Freedom Summer (1964)." *Martin Luther King Jr. and the Global Freedom Struggle.* The Martin Luther King Jr. Research and Education Institute, Stanford University, n.d. Web. 20 July 2013.

10. Doug McAdam. *Freedom Summer.* New York: Oxford UP, 1988. *Amazon Book Search.* Web. 21 July 2013.

11. Bruce Watson. *Freedom Summer: The Savage Season That Made Mississippi Burn and Made America a Democracy.* New York: Viking, 2010. Print. 281.

12. "Mississippi Summer Project One Year Later; May 31, 1965." *The University of Southern Mississippi Civil Right Digital Library: Freedom Summer.* The University of Southern Mississippi, n.d. Web. 21 July 2013.

13. John Dittmer. *Local People: The Struggle for Civil Rights in Mississippi.* Urbana, IL: U of Illinois P, 1994. *Google Book Search.* Web. 22 July 2013.

14. Doug McAdam. *Freedom Summer.* New York: Oxford UP, 1988. *Google Book Search.* Web. 21 July 2013.

INDEX

ABOUT THE AUTHOR

Rebecca Felix is a writer and editor from Minnesota. She has a bachelor of arts degree in English from the University of Minnesota–Twin Cities and has worked on numerous publishing projects for children and young adults. Rebecca has written and edited works on topics including energy alternatives and conservation, genetics, social change, and civil rights.

ABOUT THE CONSULTANT

Robert W. Widell Jr., PhD, is an assistant professor of history at the University of Rhode Island where he teaches African-American, Civil Rights, and US history. He is the author of *Birmingham and the Long Black Freedom Struggle*.